HOW TO DRAW NINTENDO® HEROES AND VILLAINS

by Michael Teitelbaum

illustrated by Ron Zalme

SCHOLASTIC INC.

New York   Toronto   London   Auckland   Sydney
Mexico City   New Delhi   Hong Kong   Buenos Aires

D0814850

Special thanks to Susan Eisner, Liza Greenwald Abrams, and Carmen Brea

A Creative Media Applications Production

Art Direction by Fabia Wargin Design

ISBN 0-439-63579-9

12   6 7 8 9/0

Printed in the U.S.A.   40

First Scholastic printing, February 2004

INTRODUCTION

MEET THE HEROES AND VILLAINS OF NINTENDO.
The best part is—you get to draw them all!
This book will show you how.

Just as it takes great patience and lots of practice to get good at playing the ultra-cool video games from Nintendo, it also takes patience and practice to learn to draw. In both cases, you'll make some mistakes and experience some setbacks. But in the end, if you persevere and learn from your mistakes, you'll reach your goal, which in the case of this book is learning to draw your favorite characters.

We'll teach you, step by step, how to draw Mario, Donkey Kong, Zelda, and the other amazing heroes and villains that flash across your video screen. If you keep trying, soon you'll be drawing facial expressions, bodies, and then characters in motion. After a while you can make up—*and illustrate*—your own adventure stories in which good battles evil.

Materials
- medium pencil
- eraser
- 8 1/2" x 11" (21.5 x 28 cm) sheets of white paper

Here are a few things you should know before getting started:

1.DRAW LIGHTLY AS YOU SKETCH.
You'll have plenty of time to darken your lines as you finish your drawing and fill in the details.

2.STAY LOOSE!
Let your hand and arm move freely. Don't grip your pencil like you are Link grasping his sword for battle! Drawing should be fun and relaxing.

3.DON'T WORRY ABOUT MISTAKES—
that's why erasers were invented!

4.PRACTICE, AND BE PATIENT.
It takes time to get good at drawing.

Let's get started!

BASIC SHAPES

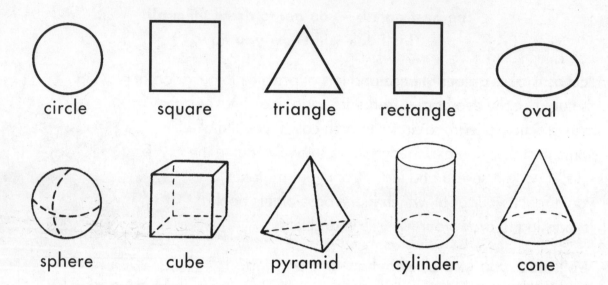

circle square triangle rectangle oval

sphere cube pyramid cylinder cone

Here are the basic shapes you can use to draw everything in this book.

All you can really draw with your pencil on a piece of paper are two-dimensional flat shapes, like the five basic shapes in the top row above. Part of the magic of drawing is learning how to create the illusion of three-dimensional objects on your two-dimensional piece of paper. Look at the circle above. It's round and two-dimensional. Now pick up a ball. It's also round, but it's three-dimensional, a real object. The trick to drawing believable characters is to create the illusion on paper that what you are looking at is three-dimensional (like the ball, or Luigi), even though it is really only two-dimensional (like the circle). Each of the two-dimensional shapes in the top row above has a three-dimensional "partner" just below it. Simply by adding two criss-crossing dotted lines to the circle, you create the illusion of its three-dimensional partner, the sphere. The same is true for each of the shapes on this page. Practice drawing the two-dimensional basic shapes, then move on to the 3-D shapes like the cube, pyramid, etc. Once you've done that, you're ready to try drawing your first character. Let's begin with the most famous Nintendo character of all—**Mario.**

STEP 1.

Begin with a large circle for Mario's head. Add crisscrossing guidelines to help you place his oval-shaped eyes, nose, and ears. Next, draw his hat, as shown. Don't forget his smile!

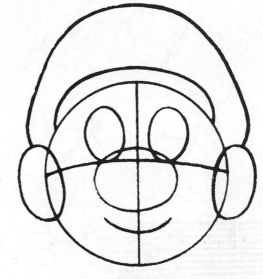

STEP 2.

Now it's time to add some details. Give Mario a bushy mustache under his nose and some curls on the sides of his head. Add two more ovals to each eye, then draw his eyebrows. Add a brim to his hat, complete his ears, and give him a chin. Finally, add the "M" for Mario in an oval on his hat.

STEP 3.

Blacken in the eyes, eyebrows, and mustache, as shown. Compare your drawing with the finished picture of Mario's head. Darken the lines you want to keep, and erase the lines you don't need. Now let's move on to Mario's body.

MARIO™ hero

STEP 1.

Draw a circle for Mario's head. Add two guidelines, like you did on page 5, to help pasition the eyes and nose. Beneath and overlapping the head, draw a slightly larger circle for the body. Then draw the arm, hand, leg, and hat shapes, as shown.

STEP 2.

Let's work on the details. Draw two smaller ovals in each eye. Add the eyebrows, mustache, and curls. Next, draw the ears and chin. Give Mario some fingers, then draw his shoes. Finish this step by adding details to his clothes. Don't forget the "M" on Mario's hat.

STEP 3.

Blacken in the eyes, eyebrows, and mustache, as shown. Compare your drawing with the finished picture of Mario. Darken the lines you want to keep, and erase the lines you don't need. Mario is ready for action!

STEP 1.

Draw a long oval for the head. Add an angled guideline across the middle of the head to help you place the oval-shaped eyes and nose, and another, straight line near the top. Add another oval for the ear, then finish this step by drawing the curved line for Luigi's hat.

STEP 2.

Time for some details. Place additional half-ovals inside each eye. Draw Luigi's eyebrows, sideburn, and mustache. Notice how Luigi's mustache is different from Mario's. Add Luigi's mouth and chin below the mustache, then finish off his ear and neck. Give Luigi a couple of curls at the back of his neck. Finally, draw the rest of his hat, complete with the letter "L" in a circle.

STEP 3.

Blacken in the eyes, eyebrows, and mustache, as shown. Compare your drawing with the finished picture of Luigi. Darken the lines you want to keep, and erase the lines you don't need. Now let's draw Luigi's body.

LUIGI™

STEP 1.

Start with an oval for the head. Draw an angled guideline to help you place the oval-shaped eyes and nose. Draw the mouth, as shown, then copy the teardrop body shape as you see it here. Add a guideline in the lower half of the body. To complete step 1, draw Luigi's arms, hands, legs, and hat.

STEP 2.

Fill in the eye details. Then add the eyebrows, mustache, and sideburn. Complete the mouth, chin, ear, and neck. Give Luigi a couple of curls. Then draw his fingers, cuffs, collar, and belt, as shown. Draw his shoes, and complete his hat. Don't forget the "L" in a circle on his hat.

STEP 3.

Add lots of stripes on Luigi's sleeves, collar, and body, and a star on his chest. Notice the details on his belt too. Blacken in the eyes, eyebrows, and mustache, as shown. Compare your drawing with the finished picture of Luigi. Darken the lines you want to keep, and erase the lines you don't need. Luigi is ready to join Mario on an exciting adventure!

STEP 1.

Begin with a small circle for the head. Add a horizontal guideline to help you place the eyes. Draw a small oval for Princess Toadstool's body, then make a large bell shape under it for her dress. Add the shapes that form her hat, hair, and earrings, and a circle and semicircle for her sleeves.

STEP 2.

Now it's time for the details. Draw Princess Toadstool's mouth and nose, and add pupils to her eyes. Draw her eyebrows and her wavy hair, as shown, including a long curving line down her back. Her arms and hands come next. Finish step 2 by adding details to her hat and dress, as you see here.

STEP 3.

Fill in the pupils with black, and give the princess eyelashes. Add any remaining details to her costume. Compare your drawing with the finished picture of Princess Toadstool. Darken the lines you want to keep, and erase the lines you don't need. Isn't she pretty?

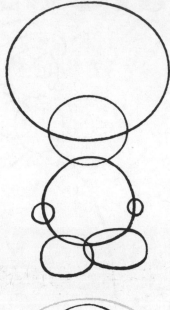

STEP 1.

Start with a small oval for the head. Add a much larger oval above it for Toad's hat. Draw a circle below the head for the body. Add two tiny circles for the hands and two small ovals for the feet. Notice that all of these shapes overlap.

STEP 2.

Draw the eyes and mouth. Then add details to the hat and costume, and draw the arms and fingers, as shown.

STEP 3.

Blacken in the eyes. Compare your drawing with the finished picture of Toad. Darken the lines you want to keep, and erase the lines you don't need. Toad is ready to go!

STEP 1.

Start with a large circle, which will end up being Yoshi's nose. Draw a body oval below the nose. Add the oval-shaped eyes on top of the circle, and then connect the body to the head with the shapes shown. To complete step 1, draw the leg and foot shapes.

STEP 2.

Add details to the eyes, nose, and head, and draw the mouth, as shown. Add fingers to Yoshi's left hand, and draw his right. Complete the feet, and draw a turtle shell on Yoshi's back.

STEP 3.

Blacken in the eyes, leaving some white highlights. Compare your drawing with the finished picture of Yoshi. Darken the lines you want to keep, and erase the lines you don't need. Yoshi is waving hello!

KEROG™

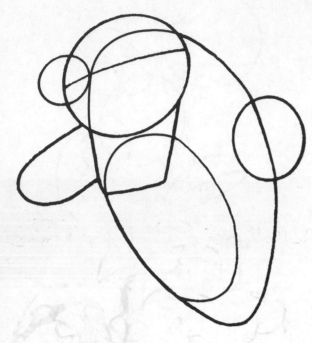

STEP 1.

Begin with an oval for the head. Draw a horizontal guideline to help you place the nose on the left side of the oval. Add an overlapping football shape for the body, an oval within the football shape, a rectangular shape below the head, and the two arm shapes, as shown.

STEP 2.

Use the guideline to help you place the eye and horn. Add two curved lines within the head oval, and two semicircles on the outside, to form Kerog's snout and second eye. Draw claws and stripes on the arms, as shown, and outline the legs and feet. Complete step 2 with a curved line for Kerog's neckband and another long one for his humped back.

STEP 3.

Time for the details. Fill in the eye, eyebrow, and nostrils. Use the rectangular shape from step 1 to form the mouth and lower jaw. Draw lots of spiky teeth, then add more spikes on top of Kerog's head and down his back. Complete the claws on his hands and feet, and add studs on his armbands and neckband. Finally, draw stripes across his belly.

STEP 4.

Blacken the armbands and neckband, and the pupil, as shown. Compare your drawing with the finished picture of Kerog. Darken the lines you want to keep, and erase the lines you don't need. Fierce-looking Kerog is ready to roar!

WARIO™ villain

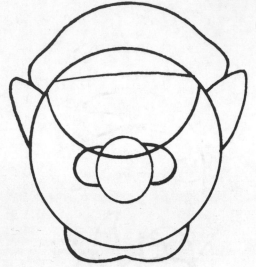

STEP 1.

Start with a large circle for Wario's head. Add a half-circle guideline within the head circle to help you place the eyes and nose. Draw a circle and two semicircles for the nose. Add the cap, ears, and chin, as shown.

STEP 2.

Detail time. Add the eyes and eyebrows, and shape the sides of the head. Copy the lines that form Wario's wide mouth, then draw the jagged mustache above it. Complete the brim of Wario's cap—don't forget the "W" in a circle.

STEP 3.

Blacken in the pupils, eyebrows, and mustache, as shown. Compare your drawing with the finished picture of Wario. Darken the lines you want to keep, and erase the lines you don't need. What an evil-looking Wario!

STEP 1.

Draw an oval for the upper part of DK's head. Now add a larger, overlapping oval for his jaw. Draw crisscrossing guidelines in the top oval to help you place the eyes and nose. Two curved lines across the lower oval will help form his nose and mouth. Add a circle for the tongue and a rounded triangle shape for the top of his head.

STEP 2.

Using the guidelines, place the eyes, eyebrows, and nostrils, as shown. Add details to the mouth, and draw the ears. A small oval shape forms the tuft of fur on top of his head.

STEP 3.

Blacken in the pupils. Compare your drawing with the finished picture of Donkey Kong. Darken the lines you want to keep, and erase the lines you don't need. Now let's move on to DK's body.

DONKEY KONG™

STEP 1.

Start with an oval for the top of
the head. Attach a second,
overlapping oval for the jaw.
A semicircle with a pointed end overlaps
both ovals. Add the remaining shapes,
as shown, for the body, arms, and legs.
Don't forget the tiny oval on top of Donkey
Kong's head.

STEP 2.

Shape the eyebrows, nose, and mouth, as
shown. Add two curls to the top of the head.
Two curved lines and a rectangular shape
form Donkey Kong's tie. Add fingers to
make his left hand, and draw the shapes
shown to make his right arm and hand, his
chest, his right leg, and his feet.

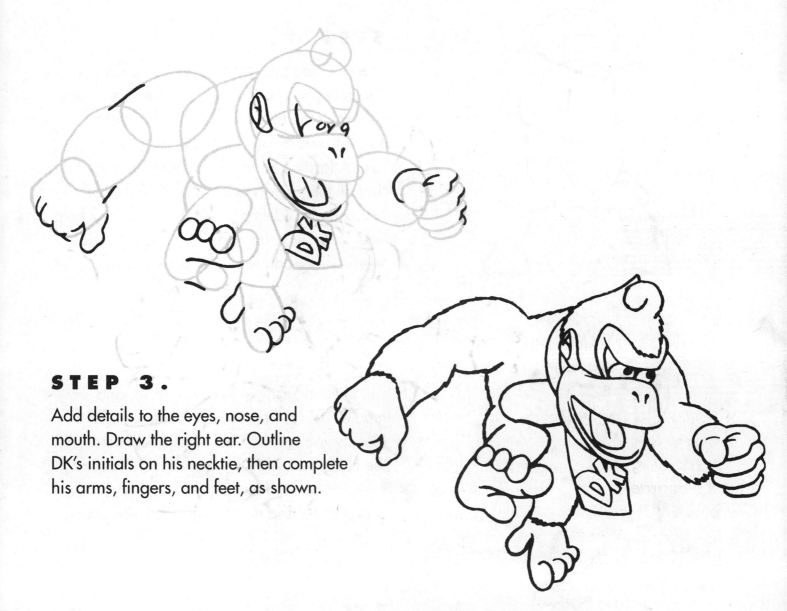

STEP 3.

Add details to the eyes, nose, and mouth. Draw the right ear. Outline DK's initials on his necktie, then complete his arms, fingers, and feet, as shown.

STEP 4.

Blacken in the pupils. Compare your drawing with the finished picture of Donkey Kong. Darken the lines you want to keep, and erase the lines you don't need. Now go over the outline of DK's body with a jagged pencil stroke to give him fur. Brave Donkey Kong is ready to swing into action!

DIDDY KONG™

hero

STEP 1.

Start with an oval for the top part of Diddy's head. Draw a horizontal guideline across the oval to help place his eyes. Add a slightly smaller oval below the first one for Diddy's jaw. A large oval forms his body. Notice that all three ovals overlap. A "V"-shaped horizontal guideline in the body oval will help you place his arms. Finish this step by adding the shoulder and leg shapes, as shown.

STEP 2.

Detail time! Draw in the eyes, nose, and mouth. Add the ears. Copy the fingers and toes as you see them here, and add details to the costume, including jagged furry lines at the wrist and ankles. Draw Diddy's long curving tail, and don't forget his belly button.

STEP 3.

Blacken in the pupils, as shown. Compare your drawing with the finished picture of Diddy Kong. Darken the lines you want to keep, and erase the lines you don't need. Now go over the outline of Diddy's body with a jagged pencil stroke to give him fur. Diddy's ready to join Donkey Kong in his next adventure!

STEP 1.

Begin with one oval for the top of the head and a second, overlapping oval for the jaw. Guidelines near the top and bottom of the first oval will help you place Tiny's facial features. Add two large loops to the sides of the ovals for her hair. Draw the bean-shaped body and the leg and foot shapes, as shown.

STEP 2.

Fill in the eyes and mouth, and shape the jaw and chin. Complete the top of her head and her hair. Draw her arms and hands, and finish off her feet, as you see here. Add the details to her costume, including two circles to form an "O" shape on her tummy.

STEP 3.

Blacken in the pupils. Add petals and a smiley face to the circles on Tiny's tummy to turn them into a happy little flower. Compare your drawing with the finished picture of Tiny. Darken the lines you want to keep, and erase the lines you don't need. Tiny is ready to have a great day!

CHUNKY™ hero

STEP 1.

Start with an oval for Chunky's jaw. Draw a horizontal guideline in the oval to help you place his mouth. Add a square shape and a semicircle above the oval for the top of his head. Carefully draw the back of the head, then the body, arm, hand, leg, and foot shapes, as shown.

STEP 2.

Draw the eyes and mouth, and add the remaining details to the head. Copy all the costume details as you see them here, including Chunky's gloves and his spurs.

STEP 3.

Blacken in the belt and the eyes, leaving small white highlights in the eyes for the pupils. Compare your drawing with the finished picture of Chunky. Darken the lines you want to keep, and erase the lines you don't need. Now, that monkey is Chunky!

STEP 1.

Begin with a small circle for the head. Divide it with a horizontal guideline to help you place the eyes. Add a small oval for Snide's muzzle, with a tiny teardrop shape on the tip for his nose. Draw a bean shape for the body, then connect it to the head circle with a thin neck. Add the arm, hand, leg, and foot shapes, as shown.

STEP 2.

Draw the eyes and mouth, and add the remaining details to the head, as shown. Draw Snide's fingers, then fill in the details of his snazzy suit.

STEP 3.

Blacken in the corners of the eyes (note the tiny white highlights in each one), and fill in the nose with black, leaving a white spot in the center. Compare your drawing with the finished picture of Snide. Darken the lines you want to keep, and erase the lines you don't need. Snide looks way cool!

KING K. ROOL™

villain

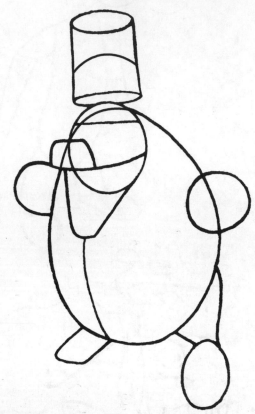

STEP 1.

Start with an oval for the head.
Add two horizontal guidelines to
help you place the eyes and mouth.
Draw a cylinder on top of the head oval
for King K. Rool's crown. Add a curved
guideline across the center. Draw the large
egg-shaped body, then smaller shapes for
the nose, jaw, hands, leg, and feet, as
shown. Divide the body with a vertical
line starting at the bottom of the jaw.

STEP 2.

Draw tiny circles around the top of the
cylinder. These will form the points of
King K. Rool's crown. Add the eyebrows,
eyes, nose, and mouth. Draw the additional
arm and hand shapes, then the toes. Finish
this step by filling in the pattern on King K.
Rool's chest.

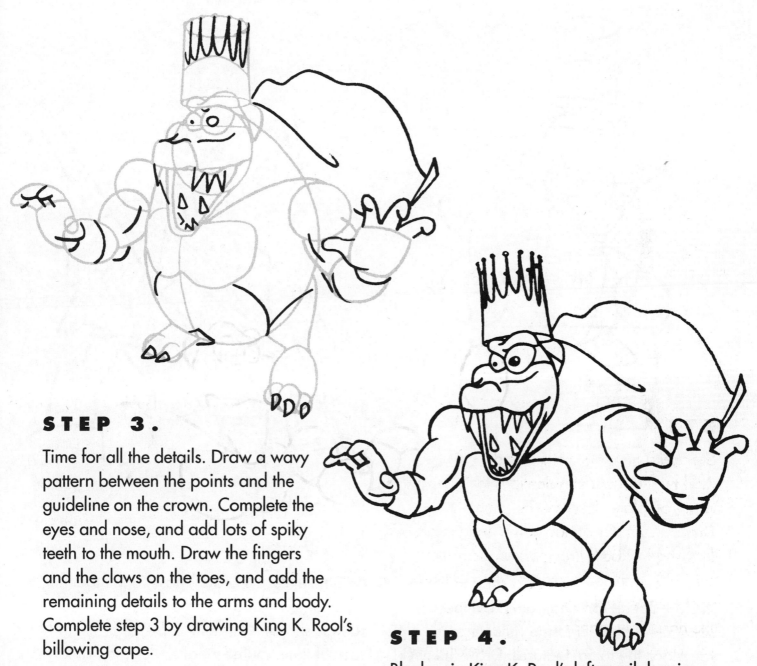

STEP 3.

Time for all the details. Draw a wavy pattern between the points and the guideline on the crown. Complete the eyes and nose, and add lots of spiky teeth to the mouth. Draw the fingers and the claws on the toes, and add the remaining details to the arms and body. Complete step 3 by drawing King K. Rool's billowing cape.

STEP 4.

Blacken in King K. Rool's left pupil, leaving a white highlight in the center. Compare your drawing with the finished picture of King K. Rool. Darken the lines you want to keep, and erase the lines you don't need. King K. Rool rules!

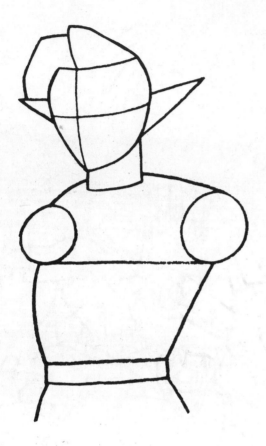

STEP 1.

Start with the head, which is shaped like a shield—flat on top and pointed at the bottom. Add crisscrossing guidelines to help you place the facial features. Draw the neck, pointy ears, and hair shapes. Then outline the body shapes, as you see them here.

STEP 2.

Add the eyes, eyebrows, nose, and mouth. Fill in the hair, and start the brim of Link's cap, as shown. Carefully copy the arms and each of the costume details, including Link's bandolier and the hilt of his sword.

STEP 3.

Continue adding details to the face, hair, costume, and sword, as you see here. Be sure to include the long tail of Link's cap.

STEP 4.

Compare your drawing with the finished picture of Link. Darken the lines you want to keep, and erase the lines you don't need. Now let's draw Link in action.

LINK™ hero

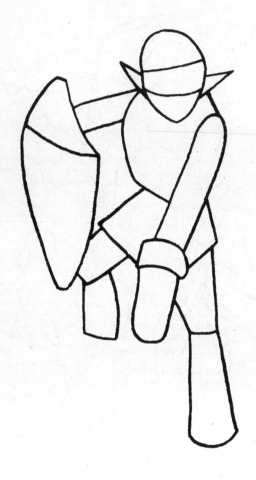

STEP 1.

Begin with the head, which is an oval with a point at the bottom. Add two horizontal guidelines to help you place the facial features. Draw two triangles for Link's pointy ears. Slowly and carefully, copy the body, arm, hand, leg, and shield shapes, as you see them here.

STEP 2.

Draw a long triangle extending out from the head to form Link's hat. Now start filling in the facial details, such as his eyes, nose, mouth, and hair. One by one, add the details shown to Link's costume and shield. Finally, draw his fierce sword.

STEP 3.

Starting with the hat and working your way down, continue adding details to the head, costume, shield, and sword.

STEP 4.

Add a row of tiny black rivets around the edge of the shield. Be sure to complete the tassels on the sheath that holds Link's sword, and darken his eyebrows, as shown. Compare your drawing with the finished picture of Link. Darken the lines you want to keep, and erase the lines you don't need. Link is ready to defend the kingdom!

hero ZELDA™

STEP 1.

Begin with the head, which is shaped like a shield—curved on top and pointed on the bottom. Add a horizontal guideline to help you place Zelda's eyes and nose. Draw her neck and two pointed ears, and the shapes for her headdress. Then, carefully copy the shapes you see here to form her body and arms.

STEP 2.

Draw her eyes, nose, and mouth, and add details to her headdress. Give her some fingers, then complete all the little details on her costume.

STEP 3.

Blacken in the pupils, the tops of her ears, and the jewel on her headdress, as shown. Compare your drawing with the finished picture of Zelda. Darken the lines you want to keep, and erase the lines you don't need. Princess Zelda is ready to rule the land with fairness and justice.

 ARMOS™

STEP 1.

Start with a large oval for the head. Add three horizontal guidelines to help you place the facial features. Draw a small rectangle for the nose and two circles to form the eyes above the top guideline. Outline Armos's horns, body, shield, and hand, as shown.

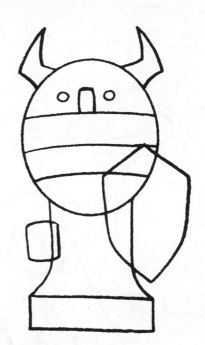

STEP 2.

Add details to the eyes, horns, and head, as shown, including a squiggly mouth on the middle guideline. Complete Armos's sword and shield, then draw lots of short lines to give his body and hand a stacked appearance.

STEP 3.

Following the head shape, draw a line around the face to give the character depth. Compare your drawing with the finished picture of Armos. Darken the lines you want to keep, and erase the lines you don't need. Now this stone statue is ready to come to life...thanks to you!

LIZALFOS™

STEP 1.

Start with a narrow horizontal oval for the head. Draw crisscrossing guidelines to help you place the eye and mouth. Add a rectangle for the neck and a larger oval for the upper body, overlapping the neck. One by one, draw the shoulder, arm, hand, lower body, and leg shapes, as shown.

STEP 2.

Using the guidelines, draw the eye and mouth. Shape the top of the head with two wavy lines. Outline the right shoulder and arm, and Lizalfos's sword. Shape the left arm and leg and the lower body, and add fingers and toes. To complete step 2, draw the triangular spikes on Lizalfos's shoulder, the scabbard for his sword, and his long tail.

STEP 3.

Starting at the top of the head and working your way down, continue to add lots of details, as shown. Be sure to include Lizalfos's right leg and his lizard tongue!

STEP 4.

Add tiny black rivets to the shoulder, lower body, and scabbard. Blacken the inside of the mouth and the tips of the spikes, sword, and tail. Give the mouth, back, and tail scaly, rough edges, as shown. Compare your drawing with the finished picture of Lizalfos. Darken the lines you want to keep, and erase the lines you don't need. Lizalfos is ready to challenge Link!

TAKE AIM, AND

PRACTICE,
PRACTICE,
PRACTICE!